the illegitimate tree

and other poems

SHARADA SUNDER

silverleaf

First Edition: 2010

ISBN: 978-81-8488-850-8

Published by : **Silver Leaf Publishing**
(An Imprint of Himalaya Publishing House Pvt. Ltd.)
'Ramdoot', Dr. Bhalerao Marg, Girgaon, Mumbai - 400004
Tel: (+91) (22) 23863863, Fax : (+91) (22) 23877178

Branch Offices

New Delhi	:	(011) - 23270392, 23278631, Fax: 011-23256286
Nagpur	:	(0712) - 2738731, 3296733, Telefax: 0712-2721215
Bengaluru	:	(080) - 22281541, 22385461, Telefax: 080-22286611
Hyderabad	:	(040) - 27560041, 27550139, 09848130433
Chennai	:	(044) - 28144004/28144005
Pune	:	(020) - 24496323/24496333
Lucknow	:	(0522) -2339329
Ahmedabad	:	(079) - 26560126, Mobiles: 09327324149, 09314679413
Ernakulam	:	(0484) -2378012, 2378016, 9344199799
Bhubaneswar	:	9861046007
Indore	:	09301386468
Kolkata	:	09910440956

DTP by : HPH Editorial Office, Bhandup (Kalpana).
Printed by : Heramb Printers, Bhandup, Mumbai - 400 078.

Dedicated to my parents
Lakshmi and
Sankararaman

Acknowledgements

For long, I thought my poems are expressions that should remain with me. Somewhere this changed and to share it became a dream. Like a dream come true, wonderful people came together to make it happen! I would like to thank each one of them and in particular:

Shobhaa De for having kindly consented to write the Foreword.

Shabana Azmi, Bachi Karkaria, Siddharth Kak and C P Surendran for their very inspiring and valuable reviews.

Bharat Kumar Raut without whose encouragement and support this book would have remained a dream.

Anuj Pandey, Managing Director, Himalaya Publishing for his support and faith in me. The friendly team at Himalaya for their help in putting this book together.

Abhijit Saxena, for his interesting feedback on the poems. Abhilash Bhattacharya for prompting me to illustrate. Zohar Furniturewala for the fantastic cover design. Bala Pillai and his team for helping with promotions.

My husband Sunder and his parents for being my strength. My daughters Vinodini and Varshini for their keen interest in my work. My friends and family for their unwavering support at all times.

My dear readers for sharing my journey through this book.

Sharada Sunder

Foreword

What is "Every Woman's Ultimate Dream"? Not just in India, not just in this century, but the world over and since time immemorial? I'll tell you.... it is to get 'happily married' and have two wonderful kids! Feminists may protest that this is not true, and that what women really want today goes well beyond this idyll. But scratch the surface, and a majority of women – even the most educated, liberated and empowered ones, still feel their life is incomplete without a family to share it with. This has been the eternal, if somewhat uncomfortable truth for millennia. Which is why, a woman like Sharada becomes a torch- bearer for today's thinking woman – that privileged creature who really and truly 'has it all' and is not apologetic about saying it.... living it.

'Sunder Majhey Ghar' was more than a TV program – it encapsulated a dream. Sharada's life does sound like a dream! She describes herself as a "poet, dancer, singer, painter." So many gifts! That makes her a renaissance woman! She is also a media professional who happens to be a chartered accountant by training! Mother of two daughters and 'happily married', Sharada's 'sunder' life has found expression on many levels and through a myriad formats. She started writing poetry at the age of 11, and today her poems have evolved into a volume that reflects her interesting journey as a very accomplished 21st century woman.

In an evocative poem titled "Anonymous Relationships", Sharada concludes:

"Decades have passed
Something still lives
Waiting to be christened..."

There is mystery and promise in those lines...

I can't wait to find out more!!

Shobhaa De

Contents

Prick of Pain

Funny Side

Touch of Life

Life Is A Beautiful Journey...

Life is a beautiful journey
Of experiences
Of relationships
Of new meaning
To the same old things

Life is a beautiful journey
Of joy and sorrow
Of attachment and detachment
Of attraction and holding back
Of varied souls who walk with us

Life is a beautiful journey
Of values and beliefs
Of conflicting goals
Of finding the purpose
Of peeling off veils

Life is a beautiful journey
Of discovery of the self!

Lost in Love

Holding Back

Away from the humdrum
The sea rocking with renewed life
Butterflies flit colorfully bright
Birds tease clouds so high!

Smiling into a searching gaze
Turning to a world beyond
Through swaying leaves green and gold
The fiery sapphire looks softened now
Kindling and awakening feelings within
I feel the sun and the heat

Almost slightly as the past returns
Its time for the fire to fade
Sinking into seamless mountains
Feelings unexpressed, set with the Sun!

The Pot Of Water

A brightly painted pot adorning her head
Gently swaying hips ruffling her skirt
Her slender silhouette on the bank of the river
Her anklets move sensuously on her youthful legs

She bends, in a veil
The wind blows
Revealing her beautiful face
Thoughtful eyes on her pot, lips as perched on a question

She walks back into the sunset
Everyday with a new offering

Years later I see her now
Beautiful as ever and grace kissed
Her anklets shine on her well walked legs
Her veil and skirt gently flowing

She settles on the bank
Caressing the stream, urging for an answer
A relationship grown over years
The pot, an excuse

Each time she had touched the waters
It was a new meaning
Today she let the pot drift away
Blissful in just being!

Journey Within

Peaceful and happy as life leads
Peels and peels around me
A gentle knock by an unknown soul
A cool breeze of familiarity blows

Deep within I know him though
How and when is beyond
Unknown to myself I am drawn
To share and care like never before

Did he knock or did I?
Kindle feelings forgotten
Together we unearth warmth
Beneath a stubborn cold

I usher the light
Through eyes gentle
Turn and walk towards life
That soul has moved on and so have I

She Holds His Smile

Their love blinds and binds
See nothing but them

Hand in hand she walked
Swaying to his gentle talks

Melted by her anger
Her nays hurt him more

Days spent sulking
He cried and pined sore

Just a tender look
Made him want to smile

Weakened by this love
He swore to be cold

Just then a glance tore
He wept to smile again!

A Known Stranger

A long time ago
Your eyes met mine
Kindling strange feelings
Sparkling eyes, a shy smile on the lips!

A bud blooming with morning dew
Leaving a sweet rosy childhood behind
Holding the new world and a new me
Close within my pounding beats

Like a dream come true
We meet again
        But sadly
        As strangers!

Drowning In Love

There is eagerness in the air
Wildness in the heart
Words pour
To a voice that stirs

Pining for a look
Anxious for that smile
Longing to hear the one
Who's playing havoc within

Torn apart by fear and feelings
Yet each moment is so full of life
Thoughts and actions conflict
Insanity is it that's setting in?

The sky was never so blue
I seek the moon in daylight
A warm blush fixed on my cheeks
A tug of love, is it?

Cherish trivial moments
A childlike spring in the stride
I stop at the edge
And step into the inviting whirlpool
Drowning

Those Eyes

The dim light hurls deep shadows
The low whispers drift to me
Tears threaten as I glance
At the empty chair across

Those eyes full of warmth
Had held mine for long
Whispering soft words
That still speeds my heart

Parting ways
Aggressive and young
On squabbles
Now petty with age

Looking across
I still feel the smile
And the warmth of those eyes

Me And Myself

Lightning strikes
Lighting the cold night
The rain pours punishing

Wet cheeks, trembling lips
And a mind that drifts back

A similar roar of the rains
The wind carries our laughter
Gentle words whispered
Warmth seeping in

A sudden shiver chills
The dark road and only me

Eyes search in vain
Listening,
Over heartbeats in pain

Tears rolling down
Make me warm again!

Stolen Moments

On a stroll by the bay
Laughter resounds
Oblivious of time and tide

A tranquil speck
Holding earth, sea and the sky
Lulls us quiet

On a will of its own
Feet take the rugged bridge
Waves lash all around
Sweeping away identity and religion

We enter subconscious and wet
Into the space of prayer and hope
Awareness of deep love and peace
Amidst the mystical mosque!

Intuition

Thoughts from the past
A moony smile

A wish in my heart
The day goes by

Lost in life
The phone sings

The voice on the other end
Startles and stirs

Remembered in the morn
I feel the grace of God

Like time never went by
Yesterday is here and now

We exist and reach out
Continents apart!

Sweetened Deception

Know not to trust
The bees that kiss
The gentle praise that showers

Know not to trust when
Love overflows painfully
While the petals open to the shining sun

Know not to trust
A promise of the only one
Never before and never after

Know not to trust
The feeling of a battle won
A victory that's handed over

Know not to trust
It's a never ending deceit
Another flower is now special!

Taj Mahal

A monument of love
Carved from white grandeur
A few cities away
In the country I live
A vow to keep

I pine for that day
Eagerly visualize
The evading paradise

Within I know its time
When we wade in
Special it will be
While some have *seen* the splendor
We will *feel* the love throbbing!

Love In Silence

As life goes by
I observe the madness
In the pace and people

Nestle in quiet, nostalgia smiles
Life's laughter
In moments treasured

Few words
Stolen glances
Fill a lifetime

Makes me smile
I know he is too
For a journey shared in silence absolute!

Fragrance Of The Night

Dim lights dance
Flickering from a lone strong candle
The soft silk pillow
Rests on flowery seductive linen

A bunch of wild Jasmine rise
Soothing aching bone and brain
The ancient gown hugs the body
Invites romance for the dance

Memoirs gush through the night
Weaving through fragrance and flame
The wick finally surrenders
To the dew of dawn!

Glimpse of Divinity

Seductive Sunset

As the sun sets lower, sinking into the sea
Clouds carry the saffron robe
Into an unknown world!

The birds melt into the fading rays
A riot of colors spark
At one magical moment all is gone
Leaving a grey lonely sky

Sounds of the wind and the sea
Wake up and make music
Unseen trees dance and ruffle
Streams gurgle and tease

It's a seductive lullaby
One that never ends
On a rocking chair
I slowly sink
Into a sea of dreams!

Do Flowers Smile?

I see the flowers smiling
I hear the wind laughing
I know the birds are singing
And the clouds playing

I move to their world
Gently caressing the flowers
Whispering to the rivers
Dancing with the trees
The wind blows away my worries

Some dawns different
Mundane and morose
I question those moments
Do flowers really smile?

Blessings From The Sun

The sun rises bright and gay
Ushering in a hopeful day
The orange rays submerge
Sorrows of yesterday

Renewed vigor and hope around
Fishermen and children charge alike
Plunging into the opportunist sea
That ravaged their lives just the other day

If it were not
For every new day
Hope and happiness
Would never find their way

Up In The Sky

Humming with the gentle waves
The perfect sky and the soaring birds
I find me along mountains and clouds
Love engulfs everything around

Come back I beckon
Into the earthy world
Pulling myself
Away from serene and still

Leaving my heart
To the mystical mountains
Some day I would return
For me and myself!

Beyond The Promenade

A sacred space along the sea
Where peace and I meet
Into the waters deep
Angst and sorrow weep

Everything around quiet
Jogging people fade
Love couples in stillness lock
Walked dogs forget to bark

The blue above, deep and bright
Makes me happy and light
For a sacred second I am one
With the earth, sea and sky

Ashram

I pass a mystical lake
Moving towards a small gate
Tucked away, almost hidden

Eager eyes search the other side
The ground opens into the sky
I tread slowly, mind a blank thought
Gentle trees and tender plants line the silence

The clear breeze fills my being
A soothing hymn floats
Stepping into a still room
Fragrance of flowers and incense
Embrace the saints on the walls

A smiling crowd of quiet disciples
Eagerly soak in the teachings

Drawn in
My soul bare to the sharp gaze
I speak words that shy from sense

Seated on my ankles
I bow,
My forehead onto earth
Ego reduces to ASH
Seeking the knowing of RAM!

Leaves From A Book

Like colors of a *kandil* awakened
Like the fragrance of a blossomed flower
Like the dew resting on fresh morning leaves

Like the song emerging from little birds
Like the words spoken through the eyes
Like a smile that touches the heart

Flowing from a little book within
Firmly rooted
Yet diverse

Like drops from the deep ocean
That rush to the shallow
And kiss your feet

Life unfolds
Page after page
Yet the book is never opened!

A Free Bird

I look back lovingly
To the years of my life
To wonderful beings that made me
To those I was destined to meet
To unique bonding with each

I thank each moment
Enriched me manifold!

I yearn to rise above
The pain of attachment
To love them all but free myself
To die every moment
To be born in the next

Like the soaring bird
That has learnt to leave the nest!

AUM
AUM

Meditative Moments

Eyes shut the brightness
The mind on an over drive
Frivolous tasks and thoughts surface
While lifelessness overcomes

Shallow breath quells the chaos
A sudden silence settles
Drowning into a vastness
A strange intensity in peace

Each cell beats
To a quaint slow rhythm
No feel of the sense
Nor the proud intellect

Deep calm engulfs
As my eyes awaken
Light filters back
Into my meditative moments!

Prick of Pain

A Thorn For Me

Spring brings the smile
Flowers are unusually bright
Dew drops are sparkling stars
I move to a world of green

I take in the fragrance
Of wilderness around
Memories of a sweet old time
When every day was spring

Running around fields and flowers
Free from fear and restrain
The world was waiting
For me to explore

A prick jerks me
The flower giving way to the thorn
I let go of them gently
Is there pleasure without pain?

A Crumb Of Bread

Life's contrasts
Conveniently buried

Has the little baby sinned?
To be born into poverty
Dragged along to beg
No food, clothes or cradle

The tears painful, a stab of guilt
Mystic answers
Let the eyes be moist
Till thou heart beats

A hungry woman and her tot
Cross again my morn path

Sprinting to the store
I return to them
The large eyes of gratitude
Fill the child's small face

She thanks and weakly walks
Aimlessly into the blind crowd!

Who Has The Power?

Unfed bodies on the streets
Elsewhere food overflows into trash
Paradox of life pinches

The unhappiness of the rich
Bickering for more

Yet the beggar smiles
With just a morsel

Happiness, thy name is power!

Stop Those Tears

Looking into the still water
I see my own self
Staring back at me
With eyes large and lonely

A tear uncontrollably drops
Perturbing my reflection
Some long moments later
The calm descends
On me and the water

I collect both and move
Light hearted into my life

Unsung Heroes

The smoke mingling with the clouds
Darkness blanketing all below
Even the pain and misery is gone
Gone into an everlasting sleep!

The thunder firing far away
Drowns the heart wrenching cries
The rain pours brutally
Everything is still, a strange peace

Trumpets signal victory
The sorrow of kin
The brave blood chill
Buried and forgotten after the win!

Stars In The Sky

Rippling waves glitter in moonlight
Grey blankets warm the sky
Trees sleepy with the breezy lullaby
A melancholic calm resides!

I gaze at the soft moon
Emotions upheave
Memories I let die
Twinkle and tease from the sky

Life, a strange journey
Meet just to part?
Take away the past
They pain the heart!

My Ghost Is Here

Near midnight it is
I settle to sleep
Looking at the ceiling
A stretch where it's peeling

The lamp lights
The face that stares
Into me from the gap

Bewildered I gaze
At the intense face
Smoky deep mascara
In and around the eye
The arched eyebrow over a tender nose
Curly locks cascade into nowhere

Wide awake I am
Not hallucinating or dreaming
Unable to move my gaze
I see a striking resemblance
To features that are mine
What's happening to my logical mind?

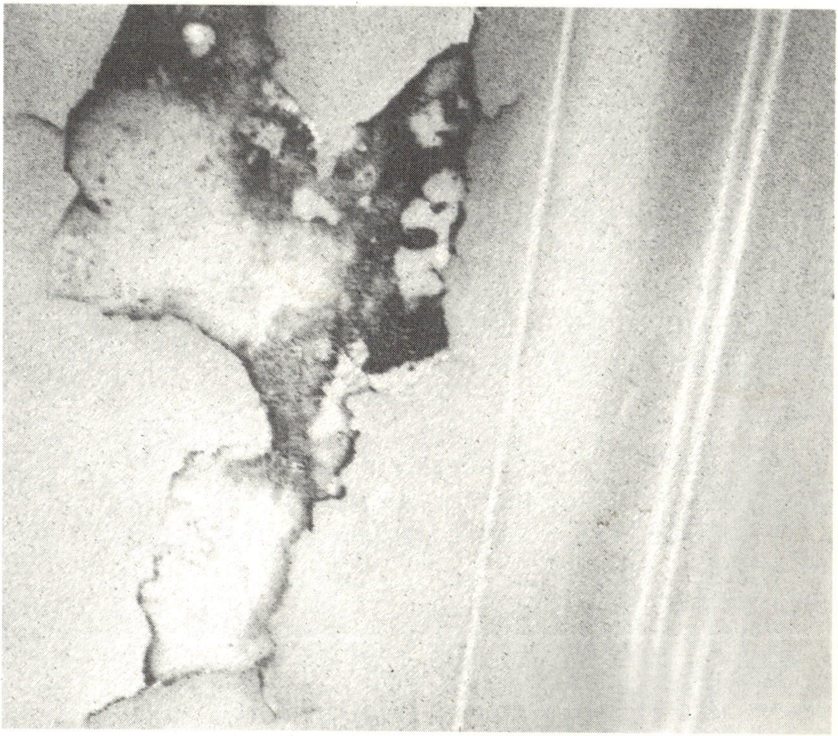

I nudge my children
To look up and tell
What can they see?

They see someone
Who looks like me!
I gingerly laugh
Lest they ponder and fear
And send them to bed
With hugs and kisses

Now alone I lay
In silent contemplation
No longer scared
I assure myself

But wonder why she's come
From centuries past and forgotten
I slowly start conversing
With my ghost who is here!

Why Fear?

Can one escape
That strange feeling
The burden and turmoil
Tenacious and creepy

No pick of caste or creed
Generous to both poor and rich
Ghostly in broad daylight
Petty yet profound

Lurking at the back
Keeping company
There is always a reason
For varied season

The mind's deceit
To reign control
To tug and test
Through frightful fear!

Twilight Truth

Just as twilight drapes
Lull of evening beckons
A still sharpness nips the air

Leaves and trees tense
The sky almost sorrowful
Deplete of all color

The parched road snakes
Sinisterly into nowhere
The birds have disappeared
And so have the dogs

A lone banyan tree invites
An eerie energy overwhelms
Oozing from its hanging shoots

Unseen forms move
Between us and above
After an eternal moment
Divine light floods the sky!

Funny Side

Many Of One

Temple, Mosque, Gurudwara
Church and Fire temple around
Prayers and mantras
Slokas and hymns resound

The Gita and the Bible
The Quran and the Granth
Gods, Saints and God men
Adorn homes and desks!

Whom does one pray to?
Who does one be-friend?
Call out to one
The others offended?

Chaos and noisy rituals
Pray tell me, HE likes it all?

Bless us to pause and peace
The one within will spring alive!

The Illegitimate Tree

Oh, none noticed the tiny sapling
Till it came up big and green
With its ruffling leaves
Multi-directional branches
We looked to see
How it came to be?

On the wall
Holding the water
Is where the roots lay
Firmly concreted
Yet needling in to gulp our water!

Little wonder then
Its growing fast and strong
But what about us
And the weakening wall?

Now starts the war
To kill or not the tree
That has strayed into our land
And water for free!

The book has its lazy flaws
On the sly we will not
More trees wasted
In reams of letters to law!

Soon the tank is drying up
Any tap reminds us of the tree
That's happy, unconquered and free
Now we have more to worry!

Shitting fat pigeons
The noisy black crows
Squirrels from the Ramayana era
All come to this new home!

Soon we will buy
Two tanks of water a day
One for us and
The other for our illegitimate tree!

Where Is The Day?

The strides are brisk
The unstoppable phones
Voice and mails crisscross

Thoughts queue up like no tomorrow
Ideas and actions brim

A nibble on the sandwich
That is breakfast, lunch and dinner

Loads of tea with lemon and without
Quench the undying thirst!

Glance at the dark sky
Laptop and file
Keep company through the night

The doorbell rings
As the pillow pleads
Another day lost from life!

My City Is Developing

The lanes till now
Lined with trees overgrown
Roads very wide
The pavements wider
A stroll in the neighborhood
Quiet and green

Now comes a whim
For towering glass
Rivers and lakes
Buried in debris and waste
Up comes a high tomb
Where waters once flowed
In there thousands toil
In uncomfortable jackets and ties

A fancy for heights
Pillars sprout on roads
Balance bridges way above
Where cars nano and large ply
Wary pedestrians walk under
In a neat file they march
On barren narrow pavements
That went under a knife

That's not enough
Now the trains need to move up
Pillars plonk on roads divided
The array of trees again makes way
Lanes below get narrower
Banners in tin, bright and yellow
Proudly declare the work under progress!

Suspended stations and trains
On squeaking pillars unsafe
Harried commuters
Enroll in moon and sky walk tutorials

Someone thought
Development was bridges,
The metros and monos
Only if at the cost of precious nature

A huge saw is at work
Felling yet another gigantic tree
That has seen decades of progress?
I do nothing but
Silently mourn
The killing of all that was green!

Then And Now

A girl smiling alone meant love
Now she is chatting into her mobile

A seat offered meant respect
Now you check your pocket

A colleague greets you, you trust
Now you look for the invisible dagger

A friend offers to help
Now it means an obligation

Gifting the poor, a well kept secret
Now it's for social mileage

A dash of emotion lent to laughter
Now calculated precision aids the smile

Some in the then and most in the now,
Perception in tune with changing times!

Poor Male Child

Obsession for male, money and pale
Passed on for generations stale
Deep rooted in minds of mothers
Fathers and the like
What's life without a son they chide

When he does come in
They pamper and prod
He is special they sow that
Taught his rights and throws his might
His face tilts a bit too high

Told what he must need and must not
Told what he must gain and lose not
Told how the family fortune
Waits for him to take on

Pleasure of growing he knows not
Protected and cared for too hard
Mind he owns not
Imprisoned in a home his own

Obliged to the special love
He succumbs to the guided path

While his sis neglected
Explores in freedom
Learning from nature and life
Blossoming manifold
Confident and high!

Plight Of Politicians

Oh, devious in disguise
Selfish and heartless
Potbellied and old
Clad in patriotic robe

It's been this for ages
The myth about politicians
The servants of people
Who unto themselves serve

Waves of change
Pleasantly charge
More people with vision
Want to now be part

Ready to take the plunge
Into deep dark waters
To swim with the sharks
Yet be a vegan

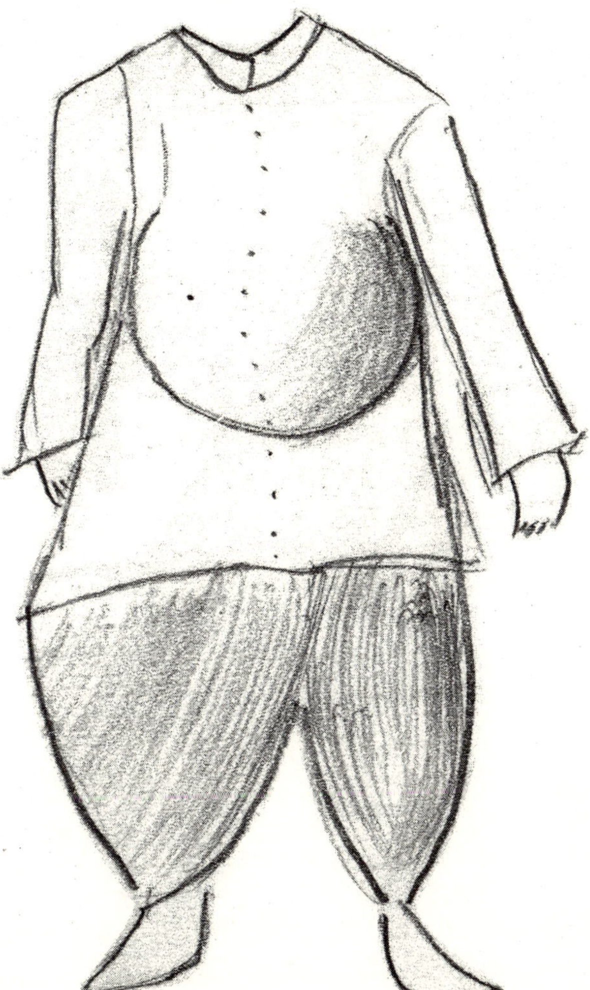

Not only sons or nephews
Bright minds these are
Who for their country care
Eager to value add

We empower these people
Fervently hoping,
May they stay pious
May greed not them greet
May nation's needs they meet
And only then
Success be theirs to keep!

In Control

The world is mine
The child joyously claims

Confident and energetic
Rising to grab the sun

Into the worldly web he falls
Responsibility and fear call

Striding now careful
Towards his dreams hazy

Life Unravels
Unknown to him

He makes his life
So he had thought

The creator drew a small circle
Said, find your sun within this sphere!

Letters

Not long ago
We touched pen on paper
Let our hearts pour
Sealed it with glue and lots of love
Walked it into a proud red box
Trusting it and unknown men
Into another city!

My daughters know not about letters
Born into e-mails and SMS
That's devoid of the soul
A thesaurus, each to their own!

Pondering in the post office
Static and untouched
I reach for two inlands
My heart opens into them
Sealing the edge with love!

I wait for the unknown man and
My daughters' queer expression
As they open their historic letters!

Metrosexual Male

With a content wardrobe
Stable and sombre
Men then used to be

Comes a surge
A sweeping change
With vengeance and rage

Colors highlight the crown
Rainbow kiss their shirts
Flowers and bees not left behind

A bright pendant slips
On smooth waxed chest
Watches and shoes need to match the rest

Sprays and perfume fill the air
A ponytail lashes the collar
A diamond sits pretty on the chosen ear

The lone dressing table
Whisked from the dame
Plain and dazed

Mirror O mirror
Your new mister
Is the metrosexual male!

Touch of Life

One Little Flower

I call it a flower
You call it passion

I see its beauty
You feel its delicate touch

I breathe in its fragrance
The aroma kindles fire in you

The brightness lights up my eyes
The colors inspire aggression in you

I see it as lending a smile to many
You think its waiting to be plucked

I see poetry in its dance
Temptation is what you call it

I see a part of me in it
You see a part of you in it too

It's still a flower to me
And passion to you

One little flower
Invoking two feelings
Am I pretending or are you?

Life In Nothingness

Drops of rain lift the muddy fragrance
The flattened soil, barren and brown
Nothing miles and miles around

Gazing into the starry bed
Hope in the eyes not shaken
Dreams and desire dance

The blank canvas, not white, black or grey
Painted with heightened intensity
Uncontrollable and intangible
The soul throbs on it colorfully

Gentle rays kiss me awake
I look out from the huge pale windows

Little spots of life line the earth
Pushing the brown and screaming green
So much life just sprout
From the dark of nothingness!

Adieu

Eyes take in the towering edifice
Memories of great times rush to tears
Just little seeds were we, noisy plants too
Grew leaves of varied texture
So distinct I and you

Learning to love and share
Growing in the care of gurus
Who would nurture
Protect and guide

The time has come
For us to move on
With a heavy heart
Etched with childhood sweet
We say goodbye!

Awakening

Dancing along the mysterious lane
Tiny feet and a twinkling gaze
Chirpy songs and gurgles of joy
Threading a bond with all and all!

Trotting on a flattened path
Love in the green, in the sky and the heart
A few steps ahead as time flew by
Was darkness in the day and melancholy in the sor

Yearning for sparkle in the smile and the eye
Blank faces, dark clouds and pain everywhere
Drowning away
But holding to hopes

A ray filters in
Tears wipe the haze
A gentle breeze with sunshine
Blows away darkness, ushers in light

Leading to a lush green path
Fresh and beckoning
Eyes light up to see
The same tiny feet waiting for me!

At Sea

One lonely evening beside the sea
Lovely waves rush towards me
With power and rhythm profound

They know not what waits
Greeted by harsh rocks grey
Recede lifelessly back

Tossed and resigned
To waves ahead and behind
Despite the conflict
Their beauty divine

On this bed of hidden havoc
Ships unknowingly sail
As the sea reflects the setting sun
I am one with that tiny ship of hope!

Sinful Expectations

I gently plant a new stem
Of blushing pink roses
Every day I care and tender
Prodding when will it grow

One morn greets a tender leaf
Elated I jump
Caressing it
Have I never seen one before?

Grows a branch
I check for a bud
Coaxing it
In zeal to see it flower

Bright and green
Just leaves and leaves
Dejected,
I move to uproot

Stopping at a thought wise
Inhuman as towards a life
Expectations and desire
Clouded my mind

I hug my plant
And kiss the love starved leaves
I no longer need it to flower!

Do You Know Why?

Why is the heart so full of love?
Why does the sun paint the sky?
Why do birds chirp with melody?
Why do waves seem so pure?

Why is there a sparkle in the eyes?
Why do I see flowers smile?
Why is the sky filled with stars?
Why is the moon so soft and shy?

Why a sad kid fills me with tears?
Why beggars linger long in my mind?
Why a caring look melts me?
Why a happy face lights up mine?

Why sufferings around pain me?
Why some splurge and others starve?
Why darkness follows light?
Why is there so much conflict?

As life ushers light
And love fills the being
I will know why!

Love Is Life

Sailing on a blue clear sea
Hopes of wealth and fame
Rise from that faraway land

He fights storms
Dreams of that promise filled land
Sees nothing than that path
Oblivious to the life around and within

With pride as his feet touch the sand
Victory's laughter unleash
Till the waves ebb

He hadn't felt the sun's warmth
Nor the caress of the breeze
Did he see the colorful fish?
And sparkles in the blue green sea?

Loving eyes that appealed to his
Didn't see the breaking heart

Didn't wonder at the starry sky
Shunned the moon as she romanced
Voice of the heart drowned unheard

Now all that's heard is a void
He yearns for all those very things
Moments tiny that he lost

Realization humbling
Hope rises like a tide within
It's never too late
To live in love!

Rainbow On Land

A beautiful island
Cocooned in blue-green waves
Those gently kiss the golden sand
Slender trees welcomely wave

On a tour to a magical spot
To witness heaven on earth
With bright sunshine and excited minds
We are a few hours away

Clouds suddenly conquer
Thunder and rain lash
In soaked spirits we arrive
Gigantic umbrellas no match

Just the grey sky and
The drenched us

I look up and pray
For the sun to shine
Even a few moments will be fine
Majestically he comes
Melting the clouds around!

The vast rocks and sand
Suddenly start to breathe
Bright seven colors
Pattern them divine

I bow and thank a force
Beyond sheer coincidence!

Let Him Be

His tiny form exhilarate his parents
Proud of his every new move
His first smile and step
Immortal in an album

Independent in his unguided walk
Curious and happy
Eager to taste, touch and feel
Brimming with energy
From dawn into the night

Questions fill his babble
Love his being

Till one day-
His parents want to educate him

The dos and don't dumb his day
Puzzles his natural cravings
Learning confined to the printed text
Old and stale like dry bread

Questions killed with impatience
Days and days, months on months
The conditioning kills something within
He tries to live, but labelled a rebel

The frenzy of compulsion looms
The smile slowly fading
Oh please please
Let him be!

Strength Of Duality

I sense the duality of nature
In the lull and the storm of the sea
In the breeze and gale of the wind

In the blue and the grey of the sky
In the flowers and thorns of the green
In the snow and rocks of the mountains

In the light and scorch of the sun
In the peace and pain of life
In the love and hate of humanity

In the way each is different
In the way each is perceived different

What I am is what I choose
Reality is within, rest a mystery

In all its dual beauty
Life is a journey

To strengthen
All that one chose to be!

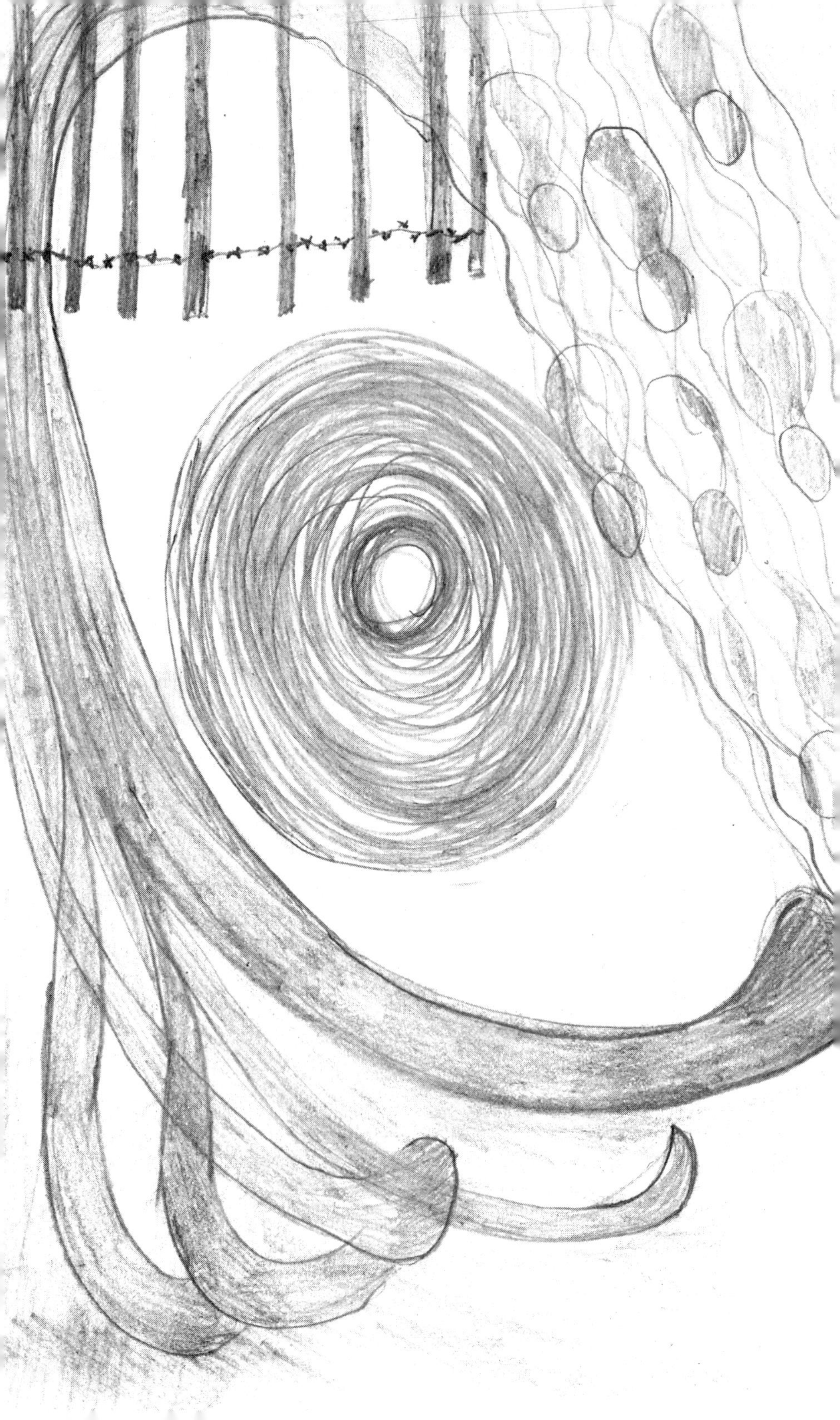

Sacred Circle

Life is flowering all around
With the stream carrying life to earth
Full of love and free of conditions
They reach the land of death and birth

As they learn and grow
Moulded by their race so old
Shedding so much of what they had
Now chained and pained in human care

A life time almost and breaking free
From all the bondage that love came to be
Peace and happiness come back

Fountains of love soar from within
Sacred and stronger
Than the stream they first came in!

The Departed Soul

Think of the joys you have filled him with
On your first smile as a child
On the first step you walked
On good deeds you did and good thoughts you sh

Think of the pride you filled him with
When you looked up to him, on your own two f
On everything you thoughtfully did
On every moment you shared a laugh
On naughty jokes only he could crack
In a subtle way he touched us all

Think of the smile that reached his eyes
When he thought of his children loving and carin
Unfailing in their duties and always there for him
Despite tides that life unravels

Blessed he felt, he gave his best
Seen his children blossom into the best
Ups and downs he has surfed
Always emerging with a smile not tears

Today he takes back fond memories
Looking back
Life spins surprises
He lived each moment, no regrets

As he cherishes happy memoirs
He wishes you will always smile
Inspiring you and guiding you
To seek and find happiness at all times!

Reunion

Studious young us
In uniforms stare back
From a black and white picture
We now compare

We feel like we did then
Now taller and heavier though
Small funny stories
Crazy and old

Fervently we share
To fill in the gap

Happy are reunions
Like a sudden downpour
Hope the sun not dry
The eyes moist with memories!

Silent Sculptors

I marvel the beauty

Of lined leaves and intricate roses
Of trees rising in rows uphill
Of shapely paths for rivers to flow
Of peaking energies of mountains

Of deft strokes on the squirrel
Of colored prints on butterflies
Of deep little eyes of the elephant
Of graceful arcs of fish so swift

Who made them so perfect?

The one that toils
Day and night
Unseen and unheard
Nurturing and holding
Setting them free
When time is just right!

My heart in gratitude
To that one and his many
Who Inspired and influenced
Guided and cared

The chiseling continued
Silently
Finely
Till it was time to let go!

Imprints On The Face

We respond to a force
In the realm of the face
The form and attire incidental

We recall and relate
Through memory of the face
Drawn to some and withdrawn from others

While the intellect notes
The color of the eyes
And the words spoken by those lips

The heart in a flash has read it all
The depth of the eyes
The genuineness of the smile

The angles of hurt
The desires held close
The journey of lifetimes

Like reading from a book
Brimming with expressions!

Anonymous Relationship

And I say it's still evolving
Stranger to a friend
Much to share and talk

To a sudden guard
Friends of his and mine spark

I won't be the docile woman
He won't, the selfless man

On a different plane we are
Being or not, matters not

Decades have passed,
Something still lives
Waiting to be christened!

Full It Never Is

Silence interrupted by giggling streams
Brightness nipped by the falling night
The charging waves pulled back
Just as the moon wanes to a sliver

Tears greet bliss at the brim
Soaring birds did you kiss the sky?
Rain showers on summer
While autumn on spring
The closer one is the farther he is
You warm up and snow settles in

Measured percentage
Full it never is
Yet we quip
We live life to the full!

A Shower

Soothing fresh drops
Soaking and caressing
Into a trance

Eyes gently shut
Consciousness just about

Tranquility and peace
As touched by the Ganges

On warm cozy waters
Virgin thoughts swim

I wrap this refreshed soul
And smile at the sun,
Happy for the light within!

Small Little Things

A small act fills the heart with love
A loving look fills the face with a smile
A caring message lights up the day
A loving hug puts the spring in the walk

A little food shared feeds a needy
Just a word of encouragement energizes
A moment of listening erases sorrow
A nod in appreciation and motivation soars

A minute of silence and nature is with you
A walk with a friend brings out the mischief in you
Little shared moments get embedded for ever
Little nothings from the past makes one glow

A little thought transforms you
A gaze into the sea gives depth to life
A little leaf makes you alive and tender
A little sparrow brings music to you

A cry of a child fills you with pain
A wounded animal brings out the mother in you
A little kiss fills you with passion
A little child fills you with innocence

A ray from the sun makes the world shine
A look at the moon softens your touch

It's the small little things
That makes life different from life!

The Dancer

Bright big eyes lined with kohl
Deep red define the tender lips
A round bindi adores the forehead
And jhumkas complement the blush

A bejeweled drape
Flowers snake the braid
Studded sun and moon above
A pair of ghunghroo at ankles tight

The music opens as she bows to the audience
A goddess-like presence fills the stage
The posture, nimble and expressive
Eyes and hands speak the story

Creativity overflows, yet in discipline
Beads of sweat shine, the body transcends pain
The face full of joy
Lost in a divinity of the dance!

Virtuous Victory

Walking through the lush meadows
Open thoughts
Sharing the past and voicing the future
Strangely with a stranger

A deep bond of trust and comfort
Devoid of power yet powerful
A spiritual connect, a beautiful bridge
To one's own self

This precious spring
Not to be lost or merged
In a fine balance it flows
Through a prickly maze

One stormy day angry waves rise
Over the defenseless spring
Forcing muck and salty sprays
Subsuming all in rage

After a vexed while
As the assault recedes
Under the pearly lit sky
The spring emerges serene

Unscathed and glowing
An integral part of life
That refuses to die!

Letting Go

The trusting mind
Blind to the tricks
The inhuman plots
Urged by insecurity

Discovery of breach
Pains my heart
Energies drained
Fighting negativity

Late in the day
Comes an apology
I search those eyes
Not trust-worthy

I utter 'forgiven'
But carry the burden
Of hurt and betrayal
For years together

One fine morning
I am finally ready
To let go and forgive
From deep within!

Petals Of A Flower

Many many people
Touch our lives
Complex and diverse
The quiet and the unstoppable

Mind if a pervert
Reads them as per whim
Defining each knot
Only to undo in a flash

No matter how many veils
The eyes and face portray
What's throbbing in
Manifests despite all

Like petals of a flower
Its fragrance and color
Speaking the language of its core!

Eternal Exams

Reams of paper filled
Heart racing rapidly
Young fingers fly against time
Inking from memory
The ominous bell rings
The last few words fill in ……. The wait begins

Animated discussions
Intellectual debates
Smoke and tea fill in the space
The project bound with unseen sweat and blood
Waits now to be judged

The grey of life touches the hair
Sparkle in the eyes refuses to fade
As experiences of life
Go through the fire

I muse
When the body rests in peace
And no bells heard
The world will judge my cold lips
To know if I died smiling!